VIRULA

I0027200

Renaissance Outlaw

ROY ALBERT ANDRADE

K
ILLER

KILLER, Inc.
Beverly Hills, California

Virula
Renaissance Outlaw
All Rights Reserved.
Copyright © 2015 Roy Albert Andrade
v2.0

Cover Photo © 2015 Ken Pivak. All rights reserved - used with permission.

K1LLER, Inc. Publishing

Paperback ISBN: 978-0-578-15697-2
Hardback ISBN: 978-0-578-15698-9

Library of Congress Control Number: 2015902382

PRINTED IN THE UNITED STATES OF AMERICA

ACKNOWLEDGMENTS

I am using this opportunity to voice my gratitude to everyone involved in the production of *Cultivating the DNA of Crime,* and the book that you are holding. I am extremely thankful for their contributions, invaluable constructive criticism, and emails during the production phase. In the process of putting this book together I realized how many people were involved. Without them, this book would not have materialized.

I express my warm thanks to Tomica Bonner, Lisa Conner, Dana Nelson, Heidi Jones, Jackie B., Sonya Gregory-Hayes, Rebecca Andreas, Bridget

Horstmann, Brie Curtis, Jennifer Rush, and Shirley at Outskirts Press. Tomica for being my publishing consultant, and guiding me through the pre-production process. Lisa for reading my manuscript, and sharing her viewpoints. Dana for obtaining a copyright, ISBN, cover scribe, title suggestions, and two custom cover samples. Heidi for aiding in the revision galley review process, and making recommendations. Jennifer Rush, and Shirley Price for handling accounting details.

I express my warm thanks to Jackie for press release distribution, forwarding media leads, and assisting me with digital direct publishing rights. Sonya for developing marketing goals, media interviews, and preparing a pitch letter for the small press department at Barnes & Noble. Rebecca for forwarding data from the representative in attendance at the 2014 American Library Association Book Fair, and supplying a sample cover letter to follow up with leads. Bridget for giving me an endorsement opportunity, and featuring my work on a product page. Brie for posting my work in a popular blog.

I would also like to thank Beth Hassid, Lydia Rodriguez, Hugo (cartero), and Victor M. Martinez at K1LLER, Inc.. Beth has always been very supportive of me, and has kept K1LLER, Inc.'s operating costs low when renting office space in Beverly Hills, California. She's the real boss. Lydia, and Hugo for helping me manage, and convey important information in 90210, and Victor for tax, and accounting services.

Last, but, not least, George Pryce. We've known each other for over 10 years, and couldn't quite figure out why we met each other, until, now. You have generated, and managed publicity for public figures like Tupac Shakur (R.I.P), handling multiple clients, and truly, a top-level publicist. You are a remarkable person, workmate, and friend. This is only the beginning, and we have a lot more to accomplish in 2015....

Cordially,

Roy Albert Andrade

P.S Cesar Andrade... Guillermo Andrade... And the rest of the Andrade's in Albuquerque, New Mexico. Thank you for your hospitality! Victor, and Maribel Rivera at Aztec Books & Internet Café for holding my first book signing. Lastly, Ken Pivak, the photographer for Virula. Thank you, all.

CHAPTER 1

Time is of the essence. In order to manage time effectively, it must be studied, and carefully analyzed. Clock time and real time are the only two types of time I recognize. In clock time, there are 24 hours in a day. In real time, time flies when you're having fun, and drags when there's nothing better to do. Real time is scheduled, and should be used appropriately. Anything scheduled, can be managed, and accomplished in a matter of time. Self-limitation, and self-defeated behavior is a waste of time to consider. Nowadays, anything is possible, and can be completed on time with an effective action plan.

I had plenty of time to think of what I wanted to be when I was growing up. In the third grade I wanted to be an anesthesiologist, and earn $100 an hour as a physician behind a beaklike surgical mask in an operating room. In the sixth grade I wanted to be a psychiatrist, and bring home a median $200,000 annual salary for providing face-to-face interviews to mental health-care outpatients. In the ninth grade I wanted to be an orthodontist, earning $90 an hour, treating oral cavity anomalies, and dental malocclusions in a shrink resistant sky blue scrub.

I asked an education facilitator, and a guidance counselor in the eleventh grade the same question, "I am thinking about joining a gang. What do you think?"

They both said the same thing, "I think you're crazy."

I dropped out of high school as fast as a high-school to pro player, and learned the tricks of the trade of blue collar crime. I built a reputation on fear, and ambition with a deadly group of people. We made money the hard way, and enjoyed every minute of it. We did everything, and anything we could to survive…

I remember, one day, Álvarez parked in the alley, and waited in the getaway car. Barrera stood at the corner of the street with a hand-held walkie-talkie, and acted as a look-out. I entered the jewelry store with Guzman, and attacked a security guard with a neon blue dead blow hammer. I knocked him unconscious, and Guzman destroyed the surveillance digital video recorder system. I shattered a glass display case, and stole $360,000 worth of merchandise. Eventually, we ditched the stolen car, and fled on foot to an abandoned house more than a century old.

Barrera unlocked the chained eight foot tall rusty old wrought iron dual driveway gate with a skeleton key for us, and we entered the property without anyone's acknowledgement. Tree roots penetrated a sewer house lateral line, and grew out from under the cracked driveway. Dead grass and weeds covered the lawn. Acid precipitation contributed to the deterioration of a roman soldier statue, and exposed black corrosive crust that developed as a result of air pollution. The apparition of ghosts and poltergeist incidents prevented real estate brokers from selling the rundown house.

Álvarez stood at a peephole positioned at his eye level in a boarded up street facing window, and said, "Nobody saw us enter the house, and all the neighbors lights are off." The home provided a haven for transients, and served as a shooting gallery for drug-addicted celebrities. I stepped over a number of empty disposable plastic lighters, and burnt tin foil strewn across the old creaky floorboards in the hallway. I disregarded the footsteps plodding along the wall, and unexplained handprints on the ceiling. Barrera dragged his finger across an old poplar panel oil painting, and Mona Lisa's unsettling eyes followed him down the hallway.

A cleaver thrown across the kitchen by an unseen

hand, struck Friday the thirteenth on an oversized calendar tacked to the wall, and a lifetime achievement award winning actress in the motion picture industry, screamed, "Wow! Did you guys see that! That was awesome! That reminds me of an audition for a major motion picture I went to in West Hollywood, and the casting director that wanted me to sleep with him for an acting role."

The award winning actress joined a small group of people huddled underneath an oval glass kitchen table, and kindly asked for help finding a vein with a gleam in her eye. An individual neglecting to attend his personal hygiene slapped her across the face, and said, "Wait your turn [expletive]."

Blood was dripping from the ceiling, and turning the tile grout burgundy as it dried up. A mysterious voice whispered, "Do heaven, and hell really exist? I don't know. Will our lives extend beyond the cemetery? Will our sins ever be forgiven? I don't know." A woman crawled out of the sink base cabinet with fatal injuries, and bruises around her eyes. She vanished, and reappeared with a sharp object in her hand. I deposited the jewelry in a custom safe installed in the concrete foundation, and shut the doors to the sink base cabinet.

She placed her arm on the solid wood cutting board, and said, "I am going to find out if heaven or hell really exists!" She slit her wrist, and shouted, "See you, later, alligator." And disappeared.

I advanced to a dark, and damp air raid shelter. I tripped over a headless body, and dropped a battery powered flashlight on the floor. Blow flies, and arthropods were feeding on the corpse. I stepped over maggots, and gelatinous goo. I disregarded the hideous stench circulating in a room constructed to withstand missile attacks, and turned the dial the correct number of revolutions to unlock the vault door to the safe bolted to the wall. I had a 6.5-karat engagement ring valued at $500,000.00 packaged in a royal blue box, and stepped over empty shell casings on the way out.

I entered a subterranean passage lit only by

fluorescent bulbs snaking 1760 yards deemed earthquake safe, and meticulously thought of the perfect marriage proposal. Dust and debris were in the air. Big-eared, hairy-legged, white-winged vampire bats made instant turns, then maneuvered to a body that was left hanging completely upside down from an alloy eye hoist hook. To help calm some nerves I tried visualization, and imagining being one of the most successful gangsters in the twenty-first century who was about to become the husband of a beautiful wife.

The underground tunnel led to a trapdoor on a busy street corner, and a line guiding people to one of the most popular food trucks in the city. I ordered a chicken breast burrito, and waited for a strikingly beautiful woman named Ms. Hanes to arrive. She is the flirtatious daughter of one of the highest paid market research analysts in the country, and the firstborn child of a demon possessed housewife that practiced diabolism publicly. Her father caught me with his social security card, a sheet of paper, and pen in their daughter's bedroom. He went to court, and was granted a restraining order.

I met the second generation college student through a member of her social-circle, and instantly became sexually attracted to her the first time we made eye contact. She held prejudiced views against gang members, and re-evaluated her point of view after an idyllic winter love affair. I introduced her to a life of crime, and cash hidden behind car door panels. My friends disliked her, because of her race, and suspected her of relaying information about our activities to our enemies. They didn't want information falling into the wrong hands, and made it very clear that they didn't want her attending any of our meetings at Elysian Park.

Nothing impressed Ms. Hanes more than a healthy young man with a higher education, and bright future ahead. She tried to encourage me to job hunt, and join California's labor market. I was dissuaded by drug tests, and questions asked during different job interviews. After all, I received an informal education from the school of hard knocks, and graduated with honors in one of the roughest neighborhoods in the nation. Her circle of friends insisted she date someone of identical socioeconomic status, and social class to avoid typical financial problems ruining long-married couple's lives countrywide.

Ms. Hanes peered over my back and said, "I'm sorry Virula, for keeping you waiting. My parents wouldn't let me leave the house with their car keys until I told them where I was going, so, I decided to walk, and had a little trouble finding this place."

"It's quite alright I wasn't here on time either," I said, and kissed her on the lips. I tossed the aluminum foil food wrap, and Styrofoam plate into a waste container bearing the city's emblem.

Ms. Hanes said, "I was discussing academic goals, and other issues with a freshmen proctor over the phone from the University of California, Los Angeles. I did not anticipate engaging in a lengthy conversation with him about my education, and future learning opportunities in corporate America.

Sorry, about that. I lost track of time."

"Stop apologizing! I completely understand."

Merchants tried to persuade passers-by to enter their department stores, and excitingly announced, "Buy one get one free," in Spanish, and English. An illegal immigrant wearing a Vietnamese-style conical hat, and chin strap, energetically, unrolled a colorful wool blanket worn wrapped around the shoulders, scattered high-quality bootleg DVDs, and shouted, "Cinco dólares… five dollars each… Cinco dólares!"

I raised one eyebrow, and said, "Do you have *Cultivating the DNA of Crime* on DVD?"

The movie bootlegger shuffled through his inventory, and said, "No, I don't."

"Maybe, next time," I said, and walked to the corner of the boulevard with Ms. Hanes.

The traffic light turned yellow, and a motorist slammed his foot on the brake pedal, creating a visible tire mark on the street. A motorcyclist traveling 75 miles per hour hit the rear end of the vehicle, and flew 100 feet through the air like a cannonball. Full-patched members of a notorious motorcycle club encompassed the car, and brandished firearms at the passengers in the vehicle. One of the members opened the driver's side door, and yanked the motorist out of the car. The man made a final plea for his life, and 11 empty shell casings dropped in the middle of the street. A quick-thinking backseat passenger sped away, and involved himself in a deadly broadside traffic accident in the intersection.

The unanticipated execution-style shooting shook Ms. Hanes' sense of security, and terrified her to take cover. She hid behind the front fender of a vehicle, and expressed extreme indignation toward the killers. She said, "Why do people resort to violence, when they can work things out peacefully, and in a sophisticated manner?"

"He didn't die!"

The helpless victim struggled to breathe, and

died lying face down. I said, "Well, things happen for a reason. He's in a better place now," and laughed. "Let's get out of here, before the cops come, and question us about the murder."

One of the most talented musicians in the history of jazz was homeless, and strumming with a pick on a steel string acoustic guitar for spare change outside an independently owned record store. I placed $100 dollar bill in a collection cup, and said, "I hope you are not going to go through the hassle of paying the America Society of Composers, Authors, and Publishers to obtain performance rights, if, I ask you a simple question, but, can you perform a song from one of your best-selling albums from 1959?"

The jazz musician laughed uncontrollably, and said, "I will perform one of the most groundbreaking songs in jazz history," in a raspy voice. He kicked aside an empty glass bottle of whiskey, and said, "This will only take a minute."

The jazz musician kept his jaw hanging, and produced a soft "hmmm," on an exhalation, then altered the, hmmm, to a stretched "ah" in his pitch. He exhaled by blowing softly through a bendable plastic straw, and I said, "That's probably been up his nose."

The jazz musician said, "Just a few more seconds," and massaged his jaw in small circular motions with his palms on both sides of his face. He placed his hand a few inches away from his mouth to feel the airflow. "Okay," he said, "I'm ready." He played stronger on the bass note, and weaker on the strum. He listened closely to the sounds of his four beat strums, and lowered his hand to play through the treble strings.

He sang a terse verse, "I view skies of blue... common blackbirds too... a helium balloon... reminds me of June... and I ask myself... what did I do? I view dark skies... stars in both eyes... I heard too-o-o-o many lies... while you dated other guys... and I ask myself... what did I do? You were worth crying for... even dying for... but... not anymore... love doesn't exist anymore... and I ask myself… what did I do?"

I started clapping my hands together, and the jazz musician announced, "Hold on, I'm not finished yet," and continued his public performance. He emphasized over song interpretation, and concluded his song in handcuffs. He was arrested for public intoxication, and placed in the back seat of the patrol unit.

The city is an allurement for Hispanic arts and culture, crowded with performance space, eateries, jewelry, and antiques on a notably cheerless block of the boulevard in the heart of Los Angeles.

A restaurateur of an eminent commercial establishment, distributed handbills advertising fresh fruit-topped cheesecakes, and said, "You will not be disappointed. Our cheesecakes are top-of-the-line, and transcend geographic boundaries. We've been featured in various magazines, and interviewed on national television regarding our delicious food."

A red-haired freckle-faced kid dining al fresco

giggled, and indulged in a crispy chicken taco without a mealtime prayer. His mother slapped him on the hand, and said, "We pray before we eat kiddo!"

The boy replied, "I know mom, but, that's at home, the guys in the white jackets, and tall white vertical pleated hats know how to cook here."

The all-too-familiar image of a woman placing her hand over her mouth materialized, and the child's chocolate fudge cake with vanilla buttercream frosting was removed from the table as a result of his offensive joke.

I took the unprecedented step of formulating a romantic marriage proposal, and said, "Will you marry me?"

Ms. Hanes was startled, and said, "I am deeply disappointed in you."

"Why?"

She said, "Not long ago, you were enrobed in a bright orange jumpsuit, situated behind a glass window, holding a [expletive] telephone to your ear, and vowing to build human capital that would lead to monetary rewards! Now, a marriage proposal... On our 29th date! What's next? Are you going to ask me to join your criminal empire, and sell drugs, and kill people with you?"

"Come on, be realistic. I'm not asking you to tattoo a teardrop underneath your eye or sell drugs at the corner of the street. I'm asking you, will you marry me."

She said, "We never discussed marriage and our future together! Have we?"

"No, but...?"

She interrupted me, and said, "I think you just received a clear answer. You seriously need to grow up, and start living a normal life. Have you ever thought of applying for a mortgage, and being a proud homeowner?"

I was honest, and said, "No, I haven't."

"You need to grow the [expletive] up," she stated.

"Where is the reset button? Are you irate, because I did not genuflect, and deliver the marriage proposal with a brilliant round diamond with a faceted culet?"

She sniggered, and said, "No!"

"From premenstrual syndrome to hormone fluctuations, and mood disorders, you really know how to [expletive] things up. Maybe, you should consider psychotherapy, and have a psychiatrist evaluate your hypersensitive reaction to a marriage proposal. A psychiatrist can develop attainable goals to help you get to know yourself better, and change your [expletive] attitude."

She yelled, "You don't have the slightest idea! Do you know what I want? Do you?"

"No, what do you want? An ultra-high-net-worth individual with a rope chain around his neck, designer clothes, platinum teeth, and a recording contract... 40 acres, and a mule... I don't know!

What the [expletive] do you want?"

She walked away tearfully, returned, slapped me on the face, and said, "I want to marry an alumni of a prestigious research university with a median compensation of $125,000.00, and owns a spectacular two-story house in a gated community in the metropolitan area. You live in an abandon house, and are involved in blue collar crime. The life expectancy of an active gang member is 21 years, and you think it's a [expletive] game. I am part of a closely knit extracurricular group, and student literary society."

"Tell me something that I don't already know, and lower your [expletive] voice. I'm not across the street. I'm standing in front of you!"

She was furious, and yelled, "You are part of a neighborhood-based group of tattooed habitual criminals that has violated every statute that man has ever created, and exchange gun fire with rival gangs day-to-day for a living. I'm surprised we haven't been shot at, yet, by one of your enemies. I know your friend was killed around the corner. It was on the news the other day."

I gave a chortle, and was growing frustrated with her. "We have enterprise-specific agreed-upon objectives, and are on the road to riches at the rate of a speeding bullet."

She scrunched her nose, and said, "You are following a predictable course. Why not join one of the branches of the armed forces? You have the option of serving full-time on active duty or part-time in the military. Make a good decision. A recruiter can help navigate your military future, and introduce you to a career-development expert."

I smiled, and said, "I don't qualify to enlist in the military, and am uninterested in becoming all I can be in the army."

She said, "How do you know?"

"I have a criminal background [expletive]!"

"What is stopping you from filling out a job

application, and becoming a productive member of society?" She asked.

"This is nonsense! I want to hire wage earners and salaried employees. I don't want to be one. In today's business environment of wage and salary rates, incentives, and commissions, people are striving to maintain their standard of living. There is no guarantee of lifetime employment, and a foolproof retirement plan. Some people prefer the self-directed path, and work for themselves as consultants, freelancers, and entrepreneurs," I said. I was irate, and wanted to gun her down in the street.

She said, "I have to meet career development responsibilities. I recently registered in an apprenticeship program to gain firm-specific knowledge, occupational knowledge, and industry knowledge. I interviewed with an automobile manufacturer headquartered out-of-state, and have to be prepared to move geographically at the end of the year in order to advance on arising opportunities. The program will allow me to work full-time at their headquarters as I work towards earning a master's degree in electrical engineering. They are going to pay for my tuition, and living expenses… We never discussed premarital cohabitation, Virula! When I move we are going to be separated by geographical barriers, and are not going to see each other as often as we normally do."

I was nodding like a bobble-head doll, and said, "I have not passed a specific nationally recognized exam, nor, display post-nominal abbreviations after my name, but, that's doesn't necessarily mean that I am a failure. I am an autodidact. I read, research, and implement what I learn on the streets. Jobholders are promoted to their level of competence…"

She said, "And!"

"And…"

Her classmate pictured as the number 1 pick of next month's National Basketball Association, dropped a water-resistant gym bag, removed his college basketball team jersey, and said, "Ms. Hanes, are you alright?"

She said, "Yeah! I'm okay!"

The ball player pushed me, and said, "Stay the [expletive] away from her."

I pulled the trousers right side pocket inside out, and drew his attention to the fact that it was empty. "There's nothing in this pocket, right?"

The ball player nodded his head in agreement, and said, "That's right."

I forced the right side pocket back in, and made a magic gesture to express that something was traveling from my right side pocket to my shoulder. "Abracadabra," I shouted. I removed my right hand from my right pocket, and gave him a hellacious beating with brass knuckles I bought from a police officer.

The ball player bled uncontrollably from his nostrils, and suffered a broken orbital bone. I stood over him, and said, "The next time I see you, I am going to make you disappear!"

She wiped her eyes and yelled, "I hate you!"

I laughed, and said, "The average career earnings of a professional athlete in the United States in a single season is more than most people earn in their entire lives... However, approximately 75 percent of professional athletes file bankruptcy within six years of retirement."

She yelled, "You're stupid! You think you are so [expletive] smart, and intimidating, you make me sick."

I couldn't help, but laugh, and said, "Your right! I am stupid! I was going to give you a 6.5-karat engagement ring valued at $500,000.00 packaged in a royal blue box, and truly believed we would live happily ever after. I realize, now, that that is a fairy tale. I raised the royal blue box skyward, and said, "I am going to donate this to a non-profit or-ganization to give scholarships for higher educa-tion to students growing up in educationally, and economically under-resourced communities… Do whatever you want… I've had it with you, and your obnoxious behavior [expletive]!"

She was furious, and yelled, "Just leave me the [expletive] alone…"

Arousal is a required ingredient in sports performance, and differs from one person to the next. I disliked sports activities, and listening to a female with a mental impairment hurling insults at me in public. I didn't have the psychological arousal to defend myself from Ms. Hanes' verbal attacks, and wasn't sexually excited to see her either. In fact, my adrenalin level, and heart rate waned like a combat aircraft shot down by a surface-to-air missile. I said, "Farewell," and gave her the middle finger.

Our crash-and-burn relationship had ended, and for the first time, I felt a loss of interest in life. '*I should kill her*,' I thought, but, abandoned the idea, and walked away acrimoniously.

I relied on public transportation, and wasn't

going to wait for the cops to arrive. I stood at the edge of the street posing with a wad of cash, and spotted a taxi cab with body dents, and grotesque paint defacement. I waved down the cabbie, and retracted my hand as she parked alongside a red colored curb zone. Painted to specify no parking, standing or stopping at any time. She tampered with the rate setting mechanism of the taximeter, and connected a device to its wiring harness to increase the amount I was going to be charged. She shouted, "Fasten your seat belt!"

The cab had a headlight hanging out, missing hubcaps, cracked windows, broken door locks, torn floor covering, ripped upholstery, and a used tampon in the backseat. "Sir, where are you headed?" The cab driver asked, and put the transmission into drive.

I sniggered, and said, "You can drop me off at the corner."

The cab driver adjusted her rearview mirror, and was horrified, "Ah-h-h-h-h," she screamed.

"What? Am I that ugly?"

The cab driver slammed her foot against the brake pedal. I collided into the hard plastic partition, and whipped back, hammering the headrest. She yelled, "Why is their blood all over your t-shirt?"

I wailed, "Dammit, lady! Its red paint! I helped paint a house earlier, and forgot to change my t-shirt."

"Get, [expletive] out of the car or I'm calling the police!" The cab driver screamed.

"The handles are missing!"

The cab driver shouted, "Get, out!"

I kicked out the window, and ran to the driver's side door. "Now, you get out," I shouted, and yanked her out of the car by her hair braid. The wig slipped off her newly shaved head, and I said, "Wait a minute... You're a transsexual!"

The cab driver yelled, "Yeah! Is there a problem?" He reached inside his purse for pepper spray, and discharged mist-like oleoresin capsicum in the air.

I laughed, and said, "Better luck next time, and punched him in the face!"

The cab driver threw the empty aerosol canister at the back window as I drove the cab away, and contacted the police through his mobile phone device. I stopped in the middle of the intersection, disrupting traffic, and shouted, "Alopecia areata, sucks! Too bad you can't grow hair, and use shampoo like regular people."

The cab driver yelled, "[expletive] you," in the middle of the street, and was struck by a motorist text messaging while driving a vehicle reported as stolen.

I tailgated a student test driver, and slipped past the express toll lane. Seconds before the automatic barrier gate came down, and avoided paying a transponder fee. I drove around town with an open container in a salvaged vehicle, and handgun strapped to a steering wheel column holster mount. I cruised down a street known as 'Skid Row,' and was excited to see a different part of the world. There were a small group of people on the sidewalk smoking weed, and clinking 32 ounce glass bottles of alcohol I recognized. I met most of them in the Los Angeles County jail, and never thought I would see them again. I drove past them, and looked around like a foreign tourist.

Skid Row had the highest level of homicides, drive-by shootings, missing children, forcible rape, cannibalism, aggravated assault, and armed robberies than any other street in the country. It had a jaw-dropping 501 homicides last year, and gang bangers we're bragging about increasing the rate this year. It had the lowest rate of churchgoers, and highest rate of atheists in the country. It had the highest rate of household's run by single mothers, and the highest rate of suicides than any other place in the country. It's probably one of the unhappiest places to be in the world.

I stopped at a back alley, renowned for prostitution, drug couriers, and decapitated bodies. I acknowledged a woman curled up in a fetal position beside a large steel waste container, and parked the taxi cab. I approached her, and asked, "Are you alright?"

She frantically screamed, "Get the [expletive] away from me," in tears. "I hate my life! I want to die!" She was in unbearable pain, and attempted to commit suicide with a revolver that holds six cartridges, but, luckily, it malfunctioned. She had deep rooted problems, and reminded me of myself.

"Suicide is the ninth leading cause of death in the Unites States. People kill themselves with firearms more than any other means possible. For example, poisoning, hanging, cutting, or jumping off the Golden Gate Bridge."

She stopped crying, and asked, "What are you… A statistician or something?"

"Maybe, I am a magician, and perform at special

engagements for a living."

She said, "That's the stupidest thing I have ever heard," and laughed hysterically.

"What's so funny? Are you making fun of me?" I asked.

She covered her mouth with her left hand, and tried to hide an irresistible smile. She said, "You are not a magician."

"I'm not! Then where the [expletive] is your gun at? Can you tell me?"

She scanned the floor face down, and in a distressed tone of voice, said, "I... Don't know! Where the [expletive] is it?"

I crossed my arms, and said, "I know exactly where it's at." I said, "Drumroll, please," and lifted the bottom of my t-shirt. I handed her the six shooter, and said, "Here you go. Please, hold your applause."

She stood up, and said, "The [expletive] cylinder

is missing… How the [expletive] did you do that?"

I laughed, and said, "How did I do what?"

She shook her head like someone with Parkinson's disease, and said, "Never mind."

I looked into her solid white demonic contact lenses, and asked, "Do you trust me?"

She batted her eyelashes, smiled broadly, and said, "Yeah…Yeah, right!" She reviewed me with a critical eye, and said, "People act predictably or by stereotype, but, you're eccentric for some [expletive] reason."

"I don't know what to say, thanks?" I stated, and flex-forwarded both shoulders.

"I really like your tattoos. They make you look dangerous, and sexy at the same time. What do they represent, and mean to you?"

An idea ripened slowly, and I said, "It represents a group of people I meet on a recurring basis, and control over a specific geographic location."

She was the aggressor, angling for a kiss, and leaning forward with her lips slightly parted. We pressed each other's lips together with a feather-light exertion of force, and closed our eyes. I introduced testosterone into her mouth, and affected her sex drive. She absorbed the natural aphrodisiac through her mucus membrane and broke away for a split second to take a breath. I gazed over her shoulder, and noticed a man acting a little strange.

A narcotics cop working on a joint drug task force led by a racist prosecutor stood at the opposite side of the alley, and waited for an independent dealer in his early twenties to arrive with an ounce of white powdered heroin worth $1,800 on the streets. While the transaction was taking place, a gunman snuck behind the narcotics cop and yelled, "Don't move or I'll kill you!"

The narcotics officer raised his hands skyward, and shouted, "Please, don't shoot!" They patted him down, and pushed him around.

The officer yelled, "I'm unarmed."

The gunman pointed his pistol at the officer's genital area, and wailed, "Where's the [expletive] money?"

The officer reached for the gunman's firearm, and discharged three shots skyward. Air resistance limited the bullets speed, and returned the 9mm caliber rounds to earth at terminal velocity. A two-month-old baby was struck on his right side temple, and bled to death in its stroller. His mother cried, "No-o-o-o-o-o-o-o! Somebody help me! They killed my baby!"

Backup officers rushed in non-uniformed attire, and fired multiple rounds at the suspects with .45 caliber pistols. One of the heroin dealers crouched down with his weapon drawn at one of the officers, and was gunned down on impulse. The other heroin dealer escaped on foot after leading two officers on a short pursuit, and tore a stolen catering truck through a crowd of cannabis smokers in attendance to see a world-renowned comedian perform at a comedy festival. A female patrol officer working barricade control for the event initiated the precision immobilization technique, and stopped the catering truck driver against his wishes to protect innocent bystanders in her tight-knit community.

She matched the speed of the catering truck, and utilized the push bumper to make contact with the mobile food truck's rear-end. The patrol vehicle steered sharply in the direction of the pursued mobile vendor's 15,600 lb. truck, and intentionally nudged the truck inducing it to turn sideways. Sparks generated like a circular saw blade cutting through a steel pipe. The food truck collided with a bright-red fire hydrant, and a geyser-like jet of water shot up into the air. The officer shot the suspect in the thigh as he attempted to escape, and made an arrest for the capital murder of 21 victims attending the comedy festival.

I grabbed the suicidal chick by her hand, and asked, "What's your name anyway? I'm curious to know."

"Ms. Brown," she responded.

"That's funny."

"Why?" She asked.

We stepped out of the alley, and I said, "I have a tattoo that reads, brown pride on my arm. I got it in prison." I made a chivalrous move, and opened the cab door gleefully.

"Thank you," She said.

"You are welcome," I said. '*Each sex has a role to fulfill for a relationship to work successfully*,' I thought to myself, and opened the driver's side door.

She asked, "What's your name?"

"Virula," I replied.

I turned the key, and recognized a clicking noise. I looked at her, and said, "[expletive]! Give me a minute." I pulled the interior hood release handle, and the engine compartment cracked open. I searched for the hood prop, and inserted the tip of the thin metal rod into the underside of the hood. It was unnecessary to inspect the battery cables for looseness, and corrosion, because the gauges on the instrument panel illuminated brightly with the key in the "run" position. I crawled underneath the vehicle, and tapped the starter's solenoid with my brace knuckles.

Ms. Brown turned the key to the ignition switch to the "start" position, and a microscopic measurement of electric current traveled through the neutral safety switch. The starter solenoid received 12 volts, and helped turn electricity into mechanical energy. The starter motor activated, and meshed with the six bolt pattern flywheel's teeth. The reciprocating internal combustion engine inhaled the stoichiometric air fuel ratio of 14.7:1, and compressed the air-fuel mixture to one tenth of its earliest volume. She hit the accelerator pedal, and we were gone with the wind.

CHAPTER 2

———✦———

I listened to Ms. Brown with a sympathetic ear, and examined her with a trauma lens to conceptualize her mental health. A Supreme Court referee awarded her $2.3 million, because she was allegedly sexually abused for years by her stepfather starting at the age of 7. The district attorney's office was incapable of filing criminal charges against her stepfather, being that, the state's statute of limitations had expired. Under present state legislation, victims of child sexual abuse are obligated to file criminal charges before reaching their 21st birthday. She was 23. However, an assemblywoman stepped in, and extended the state's statute of limitations to the 31st birthday of victims of child molestation.

Her stepfather pleaded guilty to six counts of child molestation, and accepted a six-year state prison sentence. After the court approved settlement, her attorney worked on foreclosing six of her stepfather's real estate properties to recover the judgment. The attorney obtained a nonconsensual lien, and forced the sale of Ms. Brown's stepfather's properties to ensure she was paid the money guaranteed after the jury handed down the verdict. The attorney received 50 percent of the settlement to cover her service fees, and died of a prescription narcotic painkiller overdose. Now, Ms. Brown is 29, and fears for her life, because her father was released on parole an hour ago.

She said, "I persuaded the jury with a preponderance of evidence...I was telling the truth... The whole time..." Her lips quivered, and a tear strolled down her pale white makeup. "The judgment lien was the only way to assure I was going to get paid..." Still sobbing, she added, "The law firm mailed an abstract of the judgment to the county assessor's office...And got a judgment lien."

I had nothing to cry about, and said, "Make a right at the next light."

She wiped her face, and said, "Where are we going?"

I said, "Keep your eyes on the road." And shouted, "Stop," a half-mile later.

"Oh, my God! I've been trying to find this place for months, and no one seems to know where the [expletive] it is. How do you know about this place? Do you shop here?" Ms. Brown asked. I remained mute, and exited the vehicle. She began signaling, and waved a driver around. She placed the cab parallel to the parked cars outside the store. "What do you think? Did I park alright?"

I said, "I think you need to unfasten your seat belt, and see what's inside this place. The majority of their merchandise comes from third world countries with unfair wages, child labor, and poor working conditions, but, I'm only here to buy a Ouija board that's on sale."

Her complaints didn't fall on deaf ears. She felt frightened that her stepfather would pinpoint her location, and physically assault her again. I reached for her hand, and said, "I'm armed, and dangerous. I'll be your knight in shining armor."

She made a grand entrance in a black evil-looking satin-trimmed "V" neck velvet dress with a stand-up collar, attached to her sheer cape, and black jewelry. She was maintaining individuality, and attracting unwanted attention inside the luxury specialty department store.

The elevator deposited us on the second floor, and shoppers glared at her evil horned headband. An idea struck like a flash of lightening, and said, "You are unique as a finger print."

She said, "How do you come to that conclusion?"

I said, "Just look around the store. People can't take their eyes off of you." I pointed at everyone shopping for fashion and designer merchandise, and said, "See… I told you so!"

She said, "You have a strong point," and shrugged both shoulders. "But, I don't give a [expletive] about what other people think."

I said, "Neither do I," with bulging roasted coffee bean colored eyes. "The trick is to live in an idealized state, and shrug off unhelpful criticism. Truthfully speaking, I missed out on the opportunity to become valedictorian, and president of the student body in high school. Some people may think that I am an idiot, and made a poor decision, because I dropped out of high school to pursue a criminal career. I've had to sell drugs, and kill people to earn a decent living."

She said, "That's understandable, and forgivable. I don't think there is one person on earth that's sinless, and has never thought about killing someone at some point in their lives."

I said, "Listen… I don't give a damn about other

people's expectations and judgments. They've never walked a mile in my shoes."

She said, "That's cool. I feel the same [expletive] way!"

"At one time or another, we have to face condemnation."

She raised one brow higher than the other as she received incoming information, and said, "What the [expletive] does condemnation mean?"

"If, you permitted me enough time, you could have utilized surrounding words for contextual assistance, and figured it out yourself, but, condemnation means… hmm… Severe disapproval, and some other [expletive]. It all depends on how the word is used."

She said, "Forget that I asked," and smirked. Please continue."

I used my hand to symbolize the number two, and said, "I am only aware of two types of opprobrium.

Constructive, and destructive. Constructive criticism contains helpful, and distinctive recommendations to help someone improve their lives. Destructive criticism is intended to injure, demean, minimize…"

She said, "I get the [expletive] point! Gosh! You go off the deep end, and really express your feelings with hand gestures. I like that… That's a manly quality."

A strikingly attractive woman in a dry cleaned long sleeve single button notched collar jacket with flap pockets at the waist, and pleated flared-hem skirt introduced herself as a sales associate. "Is there anything I can help you with today, handsome?"

Ms. Brown had become defensive, and said, "Handsome," with closed fists.

I reached for Ms. Brown's hand, and said, "I want to purchase a Ouija board, but, I am having trouble finding one. Can you help us?"

The sales associate placed her hands on her hips,

and said, "I will be more than happy to help you find one. Are you a VIP member? If, so, you are entitled to 50% off all our merchandise, and 12 months of 0% annual percentage rate on all purchase. This offer expires today."

"No, I'm not a VIP member. I am a gang member."

Ms. Brown looked at me, and said, "What the [expletive] does that have to do with anything?"

"I was only joking around."

The sales associate turned around, looked back over her shoulder, and said, "Please, follow me. I will direct you to our psychometry department."

"Lead the way," I stated with an extending arm level to the ground.

The sales associate said, "We are a premier luxury retailer offering premium assortments of attire, beauty, jewelry, accessories, and ornamental home products to affluent consumers, who earn more than $125,000 a year, and possess liquid assets of at least $250,000."

I consciously bumped into a shopper in a single-breasted black tuxedo jacket, and made him spill a half-full glass of champagne on the sales floor.

"Watch where the [expletive] you're going, 007!"

His wife nudged him, and said, "Don't just stand there. Do something!"

He became incensed, and said, "What the [expletive] do you want me to do, sue him?"

She yelled, "Call the police."

He said, "For what?"

She said, "For what? An assault, and battery! You're the lawyer, you figure it out."

He said, "Some states combine assault, and battery as a single offense. In spite of that, I don't think there is much the police can do, but, write a report, and a background check."

The sales associate walked around a 32 inch wide platinum plated frame, and tempered glass display case above an intricate design pillar stand, and said, "You're in luck. We have one in stock... The Ouija board was invented around the time Thomas Jefferson became the third president of the United States of America."

I remarked, "If, I remember correctly, the towering sandy-haired, freckled, politically credentialed 57-year-old man, is the only U.S president to walk to, and from his inaugural, which, I believe was on March 4, 1801."

The cashier covered the Ouija board with bubble cushioning wrap to provide a combination of surface protection, and void-fill, before placing the spirit board in a rectangular box filled with petroleum-based polystyrene peanuts. She said, "And, how will you be paying for your purchase today? Cash, debit, or credit, sir?"

I handed her an anodized aluminum payment card, and said, "A man in his 30s had his debit card stolen, and decided not to report the incident to the police, because the thief spent less money throughout the day than his wife."

The cashier didn't laugh. Ms. Brown said, "I thought it was funny.

The cashier gazed over the credit card, and said, "You have to have a blemish-free credit history, and ridiculous net worth to be carrying around this type of credit card. Are you self-employed?"

"Something like that."

The cashier fictitiously swiped the card through the payment terminal, and said, "The countertop device should bring us to a home screen, which reads, sale, refund, and void, and give us two options to choose from. Debit or credit. However, our point-of-sale equipment is unable to read the magnetic strip on the back of your card."

'*I knew this was going to happen*,' I mentally stated. "You can still accept the payment card, but, must run the transaction by keying in the card's information," I said.

The cashier scratched his head, and said, "We signed a merchant agreement to accept these type of invitation-only charge cards, but, I need to contact a retail floor manager to complete the transaction. Do you mind waiting?"

"No, not at all. Take your time, dude."

Ms. Brown said, "Virula! What's going on?"

"This narrow-minded buffoon is questioning the legitimacy of the individual presenting the invitation-only charge card."

She said, "Who, you?"

I gave her a nonverbal sign of agreement, and said, "He is going to keep the card in question in hand, and alert their high end security officers."

She said, "What are we going to do?"

With a brooding frame of mind. I said, "Relax! Everything turns out right in the end."

The cashier picked up the phone, and acted like he was trying to contact the floor manager. He forewarned the bank that he may have a fraudulent transaction, and covered the handset microphone with the palm of his hand. "Mr. Virula! I'm still trying to get ahold of the floor manager. I apologize for the inconvenience."

"Not a problem. Thank you," with a thumb thrust skywards. "We're not going anywhere," and briefly closed one eye as a sign of bonhomie.

The cashier responded to a series of 'yes' and 'no' inquires over the phone, and attempted to determine if the card was valid. He whispered, "I did everything I could to protect your cardholder, and service establishment from identity theft... Unfortunately, a painted out signature panel, and re-embossed account number is unapparent... No... The ink on the raised card number, name, and expiration date is not blotted... Thanks again... I will... Goodbye!"

The cashier placed the phone down, and said,

"Things can get a little complicated around here." He pressed F2 on the countertop device's home screen, and entered the embossed bank card number manually. He entered the expiration date, and hit 'enter.' The device prompted him for the amount of the transaction, and said, "A sales tax is imposed on all state retailers, and pertains to all retail sales in our city. Your total is $1,800.50."

The employee asked for a zip code. I proudly stated, "91331."

I signed the first receipt printed, and set the customer copy on fire with a disposable lighter, featuring artistic Aztec cultural patterns inspired by tattoo artwork. Ms. Brown erected her thumb, index, and middle finger. "There are three elements required to start a fire... Fuel, oxygen, and heat. Fuel is required for the fire to burn. Oxygen is essential for the fire to breathe. And heat is necessary for the fire to sustain burning."

I chuckled, and said, "Who the [expletive] do you think you are, Smokey the Bear?" An agreeable, laughter-provoking emotion enkindled, and I shouted, "Stop! I'm ticklish."

She said, "You're too serious! Lighten-up!"

I was teary-eyed, and said, "Okay, I get the picture, now, stop tickling me."

A livid-faced loss prevention specialist suspected us of external theft, and stopped us in our tracks. He raised his hand above shoulder height with the palm facing us, and said, "Wait, a minute! Do you have a receipt?"

"No!"

The loss prevention specialist said, "According to a survey, shoplifting accounts for approximately $13.5 billion in yearly losses for retailers nationwide."

"So, what the [expletive] does that have to do with us?"

The loss prevention specialist said, "I need to verify your purchase."

"No, you don't," with clenched fists.

The loss prevention specialist said, "Yes, I do," and used his body to block the exit.

I looked at Ms. Brown, and said, "Watch this. I'm going to knock this [expletive] out cold."

I stretched one arm 2 inches short of its full extension, and sent his nervous system into a state of temporary paralysis. I stood over him, and said, "No, you don't."

An entry-level employee attempted to shoo shoppers holding cell phone cameras out of the walkway, but, they stopped at nothing to snap a picture of the loss prevention specialist, lying unconscious on the floor, and joked about uploading his image on their favorite social networking websites.

We exited the luxury specialty department store, and viewed a patrol officer circling the taxicab with a Traffic Notice to Appear book. I walked up to her, and said, "Come on lady, I'm a taxpayer."

The patrol officer said, "You are being cited for having a cracked windshield, and not displaying rates on the meter."

I had a strong urge to cast insults at the citing officer, and yelled, "[expletive] you!"

The officer finished writing her name, and the vehicle code violation on the ticket. "Here, you go!"

I read the codes, and section numbers, laughed, and said under my breath, "I will use this ticket for toilet paper."

I was issued a second citation for cracked windows, exterior, and interior dents. I said, "[expletive] you, you [expletive] dyke!"

The patrol officer smiled, and said, "Oh, yeah."

"Yeah!"

The patrol officer issued a third citation for noticeable fluid leaks, grimed upholstery, and a used tampon in the backseat. She said, "Here you go," and handed me the citation.

I laughed hysterically, and said, "I don't even care. That's not my car."

We hugged and kissed, again, like Romeo and Juliet's first kiss. The heart-healthy micro workout dilated blood vessels, and lowered our blood pressure. I unlocked my lips, and said, "Intimate space expands externally from our soul case, 46 centimeters in every direction, and indicates a closer relationship."

Ms. Brown said, "Shut up, and kiss me, Virula!"

I placed her hair behind her ears, and looked her romantically in the eyes. She muttered, "I love a man that's chivalrous, and fearless at all times. It turns me on." The smooch-a-thon increased levels of oxytocin, and heightened our immunity.

An elderly man leaning on his cane at the corner raised a megaphone, and shouted, "Carbon pollution is causing visibility impairment, and all sorts of health problems... the end is near... if, this continues we will undergo poorer air quality... diseases are spreading through food, insects, and water at an alarming rate... Envision food shortages among other consequences. We must act now, or else our offspring are headed for disaster... an environmental bill needs to be passed by the state legislature, and signed by the governor to force the state board into adopting a statewide greenhouse gas emissions limit."

"Man! That old [expletive] is crazy, and needs to learn how the legislative process works, before, he opens his big mouth, and alarms people about pollution. He needs to contact senators, and assembly members that represent Californians to get [expletive] done the right way... His ideas can influence a senator or assembly member to author a bill, but, he's not going to accomplish anything standing at the corner of the street with a megaphone, and waiting for people to honk their horns to show their support."

Ms. Brown's eyes widened. "That's interesting. I never thought of that, Virula."

A dog approached a bitch on the sidewalk, and used his paws to grasp her hip bones, and penetrated her vulva. Her vulva contracted around his bulbus glandis, and the two became inseparable. I looked away, and said, "Venus is the hottest planet in our solar system. Northeastern Siberia consists of 3 people per square kilometer, and is possibly considered the coldest inhabited place on Earth."

Creases ran from the side of her nose to the corner of her mouth. "You're funny. Do you know that?"

I looked at her, and said, "No, I was unaware of that."

She said, "Why should I be concerned about something as unexciting as air pollution?"

"Well, air pollution containing high-levels of benzene, and vinyl chloride can lead to birth defects, cancer, nerve, and brain damage."

She stopped, and said, "What is benzene?"

"A highly flammable colorless chemical used to manufacture detergents, plastics, pesticides, dyes, and drugs."

Then she said, "What is vinyl chloride?"

"Hmm! I don't want to go into details, but, it's one of the highest production volume man-made substances in the [expletive] world."

We walked from the hoity-toity to the hoi polloi. As twilight set in on the afternoon, sidewalks buckled, broken, and twisted by tree roots, filled with toothless, and shoeless happy-go-lucky locals drinking wine, and injecting drugs into their bloodstreams, sharing needles with people who were HIV positive. Some were mumbling to themselves, while others were shouting vulgar language into the air, and pushing shopping carts overloaded with their worldly possessions.

A wheelchair-bound man at the street corner deposited steel wool at the end of a pencil-width air tire pressure gauge to hold a rock of off white crack cocaine in place. He used a lightweight self-igniting micro torch to heat the powerfully addictive drug until it liquified, and inhaled the vapors into his lungs through the opposite side of the tire gauge. He experienced abdominal pain, and said, "I need to raise more money."

"For what," I asked.

He said, "To buy more crack," and laughed demonically. Holding a crumpled cardboard sign asking motorists for money, he shouted, "I was cited for panhandling, and violating a state statute that bans soliciting near roadways. That's unfair. Especially, for a drug addicted buffoon like myself that needs to get high every day, and beg people for money on an empty stomach. [expletive] work!"

The wheelchair-bound man pointed his finger at me. "Will you help me?"

"Sorry, but, I am living on a fixed income, and creating a budget to stay ahead of inflation."

The man said, "That's alright. There's a sucker

born every minute."

"That phrase is linked to Phineas Taylor Barnum, a legendary European American businessman of the 19th century," and continued walking. I glanced at Ms. Brown. "Do you want to know something interesting?"

Ms. Brown shook her head up, and down. "Yes, I do."

"Dr. Richard J. Gatling invented one of the earliest rapid-fire weapons in history to reduce the size of armies, and patented his invention in 1862."

She said, "What the hell made you start thinking about guns right now? Is something bothering you?"

I noticed a homeless man in unwashed ill-fitting clothes pick up a half-smoked cigarette off the ground, and use a sidewalk shrine to relight the cigarette. I turned my attention over to Ms. Brown, and explained, "No, I've always had a fascination with guns."

Ms. Brown's eyes bulged. "You're one knowledgeable [expletive]. I am impressed."

"It comes from two things."

"What's that?" She said.

"Experience, and education."

An army veteran ripped a page out of the Bible, and tactfully placed loose tobacco evenly on the thin grade of paper. He twisted the paper evenly between his thumbs and forefingers. He licked one side to keep the paper together, and shouted, "All I need now is a light! Does anyone have a light? I repeat, does anyone have a lighter?"

I stopped, and said, "Here you go!"

I handed him, what appeared to be a conventional push-button lighter, but, it was actually an electric shock lighter, I had turned to shock mode. A stray dog lifted his back leg, and urinated on the brick wall. The veteran with the Bible rolled cigarette stood barefoot in urine, and thanked me for the lighter. He rotated the spark-wheel, and pushed down on the fork using his thumb. He collapsed, and began twitching.

An emergency medical technician saw him on the sidewalk, and shouted, "Stop, the vehicle!"

The medical technician sprinted to the army veteran with an automated external defibrillator, and asked, "Are you okay?" The veteran was unresponsive, and bleeding from the back of his head. The technician said, "C-A-B... Circulation... Airway... Breathing! I got it!" He measured three finger widths from the bottom of the sternum, and placed one hand above the other in the center of the army veteran's hairy chest. He utilized his upper body weight to compress the chest approximately 4.9 centimeters in the hoary haired man, and pushed at a rate of 99 compressions a minute.

The ambulance driver ran over to his co-worker, and said, "Cardiopulmonary resuscitation consists of chest compressions, and mouth-to-mouth breathing."

The medical technician asked him, "Do you want to pinch his nostrils, and breathe a few short breaths into his mouth?"

The ambulance driver noticed the veteran's tooth discoloration, and said, "No way Jose!"

The medical technician said, "Then shut the [expletive] up then." He tilted the veteran's head back, and scrutinized him for chest motion. "Dammit! This can't be happening! We need to save his life."

The ambulance driver said, "Why, so he can get high again?"

The medical technician closed the veteran's mouth, and said, "Breathing into a victim's mouth doesn't always work," then covered his nostrils with his mouth, making a seal, and inflated his lungs with three rescue breaths. "Cardiopulmonary resuscitation can help oxygenated blood travel to the organ that serves as the center of the nervous system, and a few other vital organs to restore a normal heart rhythm. A human can still be revived within 7 to 11 minutes after the heart stops."

The veteran was gasping for air, and the medical technician said, "Here goes nothing!" He used a disposable razor with multiple blades to trim the army veteran's chest hair down, and listened to voice prompts that enabled him to use the automated external defibrillator correctly. He placed two pads with electrodes to the army veteran's chest, and depressed the "analyze" button. He was given step-by-step instructions as the device checked the army veteran's heart rhythm, and directed him to press the automated external defibrillators "shock" button.

The electric shock caused the heart to pump blood, and restore a conventional rhythm. The army veteran bent his knees towards his chest, rolling back to his shoulders, and leveled his hands on the concrete. He forced his legs away from the sidewalk, and landed on both feet. He asked the emergency medical technician, "Who the [expletive] are you?"

The ambulance driver placed his arm around his colleague's shoulders, and said, "This man saved your life!"

The veteran performed a two-foot high kick within eyeshot, and left the paramedics motionless on the edge of the sidewalk.

Ms. Brown and I crossed the street, and paused in front of a Googie-style coffee shop. We marveled at the upswept roof, geometric shapes, starburst shapes, and neon lights. An hourly wage employee exited the coffee shop to enjoy her 15-minute paid rest break. As I gazed up at the restaurant the hourly wage employee said, "It's breathtaking, isn't it?"

"You got that right," I stated.

The employee said, "The building was constructed in the 1950s and represents America's fascination with space. This is a popular destination for Hollywood movie stars, and movie producers for their morning coffee."

Ms. Brown said, "That's bloggable."

I carefully studied the menu option, and ordered two cups of the rarest gourmet coffee beverage in the nation. A highly skilled barista handcrafted our beverages, and said, "That'll be $216.50."

Ms. Brown began glowering, and said, "That's absurd! Are you buying coffee for everyone or what?"

"No, what are you talking about? Relax! Sales tax is 8.25. Total tax is 16.50. Just find us a seat." I smiled at the barista, and said, "She's never had this kind of coffee before, and is unaware of its market value." I handed the highly skilled barista 3 hundred-dollar bills, and said, "Keep the change."

The barista was radiant, and said, "Thank you, sir!"

I pulled up a barstool with white upholstery to a round pub table, and sat in a 21 inch bucket seat. I said "This coffee gets its savor from the ripest coffee berries a lithe-bodied wild animal consumes, and then excretes in its stool. The coffee cherries go undigested by civet cats, thus making it workable for civet-coffee farmers to store, and process speedily to prevent spoilage."

Ms. Brown asked, "Is that possible?"

"The hand-gathered civet coffee beans that are mixed with feces are minutely washed, and slightly roasted after being dried out in the sun."

She compressed her eyes, and said, "That's disgusting. I'm not drinking it. Can't you think of anything else to talk about other than an animal's digestive tract, and predigested coffee extracted from civet feces? Today, is Father's Day!"

I raised one eyebrow higher than the other, and asked, "Today's Father's Day?"

She nodded her head, and said, "Yep!"

I paused, and said, "I'm fatherless!"

She said, "Why?"

"A call-taker at the police department received

a call concerning domestic violence, and dispatched a patrol unit to our place of residence. Well, when the police arrived, the old man greeted them with gunfire, and then turned the gun on himself."

She said, "That's horrible. I'm sorry to hear that."

"Don't be! I was taken to the hospital with more than 21 different injuries. I had contusions, and breathed oxygen through a ventilator for 72 hours."

She used her hands to cover her mouth, and said, "Oh, my God! How old were you?"

"7."

She asked, "How old are you now."

"22."

She said, "That happened 15 years ago."

"Child abuse materializes at each step up the socioeconomic ladder, beyond ethnic groups and cultural boundaries, within world religions, and at all levels of educational attainment. So, [expletive] happens," I stated.

A tear streamed down Ms. Brown's milk white mascara, and I said, "In 1914, a Father's Day resolution was passed by Congress in honor of America's fathers. In 1972, U.S President Richard Nixon requested that the third Sunday of June be recognized as Father's Day... I dislike the unmanliness of gift-giving, and the commercialism of the whole idea of Father's Day!"

She wiped her tears, and said, "That's understandable. You're a man."

"Let's get out of here," I said.

We left two full cups of civet-coffee on the round pub table, and ambulated to a 40-mile formal bicycle trail alongside white water rapids, bubbling between concrete-lined flood-control channels. We walked to one side to allow horseback riders, joggers, bicyclists, and a surveyor with an infrared reflector used for distance measurement, to pass.

We crossed a historical bungee-jumping venue, and I said, "This is the county's oldest standing bridge, and its experiencing concrete degradation due to a chemical process known as alkali-silica reaction. It's already creating micro-cracks in the concrete."

CHAPTER 3

———————

We stood in front of a chained eight foot tall rusty old wrought iron dual driveway gate. Ms. Brown asked, "Why are we here?"

"I live here!"

She pointed at the 13,000-square-foot house, and said, "You-u-u-u, live here!"

I gazed at the dilapidated terracotta-hued barrel clay roof tiles, and said, "I sure do! Why?"

She said, "This place is haunted."

"How do you know?"

Her arteries dilated, and her blood pressure dropped. She laughed uncontrollably, and said, "Word of mouth." I removed a stainless steel tension wrench and tempered carbon steel pick tucked behind a global positioning system monitoring device tethered around my ankle. She asked, "What the [expletive] is that?"

"These are professional locksmith tools."

She tittered. "No, stupid!" And pointed at the GPS ankle monitor. "That!"

I took a deep breath, and admitted, "I was recently released from custody, and am now under post-release community supervision. Taxpayers aren't so happy about it, since, it's manufactured at their expense, and hard earned dollars, but, what can I do? The probation officer wants to monitor me around the clock!"

She said, "Honesty is the best policy."

I smiled, and said, "Give me a minute."

I used the tension wrench to apply rotational pressure on the padlock, and used the pick to press the pins up, and down. I opened the gate, and said, "Ladies first."

She glanced at the tree-lined, and shaded streetscape. Then gaped at the long private drive-way, ending at a motor court, and water fountain. "Here goes nothing."

"You won't be disappointed," I said, and re-locked the eight foot tall rusty old wrought iron dual driveway gate.

An odorant stimulated the chemoreceptors in Ms. Brown's nose, and conveyed electrical impulses to her brain. She said, "What's that smell?"

I looked at her, and said, "I don't know."

Álvarez opened the unfinished mahogany two-panel plank entry door, and said, "Hurry up! And watch your step!"

He peeled back a premium virgin wool blanket,

and revealed a body's legs cut off at the knees. Ms. Brown fainted, and I said, "What's the big idea?"

Álvarez said, "It was Castillo's idea!"

"Castillo! What the [expletive] is he doing here?"

He said, "I don't know!"

"Where the [expletive] is he at?"

Álvarez murmured, "He's in the dinette."

"Take her to Andrade's bedroom."

Álvarez hesitated, and said, "But…"

"Just do it!" I bawled.

I found another victim laying lifelessly in the hallway with duct tape over his mouth, and dismembered parts of his body cooking on a single burner portable gas stove in the kitchen. Castillo was surprised to see me, and dropped his spatula on the floor. "Virula! How are you? Long time no see."

"I've been working like a dog, and burning the candle at both ends."

Castillo displayed a genuine smile, and said, "It's good to see you."

I said, "Likewise," as he released his arms from a non-sexual hug. "The Aztecs engaged in cannibalistic behavior to placate their gods… The meat yield from the median human being provides around 3.9 kilograms of protein, therefore, meeting the day-to-day nutritional demands of merely 59 adults."

"I am enamored with eating people. I love cutting, and removing the meat from a skeleton. It's sexually exciting," Castillo stated.

"You really have a psychopathic personality."

Castillo was in a euphoric state of mind, and said, "On, May 14, 1607, English settlers established the first British settlement in the Western Hemisphere, namely, Jamestown, Virginia of North America. They arrived aboard three ships." He signified the number three with his index, middle, and ring fingers in silent dialogue. "The Discovery, the Susan Constant, and the Godspeed. Archaeologists disclosed their research of 17th century skeletal remainders advocating that English settlers exercised cannibalism to remain alive."

"That's partially true. I think the Jamestown colonists had difficulty growing crops, and experienced a harsh winter known as the Starving Time. I'm not doubting you. Their food supply came from England. May I remind you that we are living in the 21st century? Hybrid powered cars, robotics, human cloning, automation, nanotechnology, genetic engineering, artificial intelligence, hypersonic transportation, and supermarkets exist."

Castillo said, "[expletive] you," in a belligerent tone and an artillery bombardment ensued. Bullets pinged and ricocheted around me. He pressed the black button on the side of the hand grip, and ejected a 10-round limit 9mm magazine. "You can run but you can't hide," He shouted. He pushed the tenth cartridge toward the back of the hardened steel tube, and slid the magazine into the hand grip. The magazine locked in place, and he yelled, "I'm going to kill you!"

Álvarez entered the kitchen at the speed of light, and shouted, "Virula is hiding in the closet!"

Castillo shouted, "Come out, come out, wherever you are."

He fired 10 holes through the closet door, and said, "I'm sorry it had to end this way."

I tapped him on his shoulder, and said, "I do too."

I pulled the trigger, and shot him in the back of the head. Álvarez cheerfully dragged him to a bathtub full of water, hydrochloric, alkaline hydrolysis and muriatic acid to flush him down the drain. Álvarez said, "He faced an enormous challenge in returning from a psychiatric hospital, and having to re-assimilate back into society. Now, he's dead, and will be on his way to the largest water treatment facility in the world in 3 days."

"It can take up to 13 hours for his muscles, and cartilage to completely dissolve. His bones should turn into dust within 3 days. We'll destroy 99 percent of the evidence."

Álvarez asked, "What about the 1 percent?"

I glanced around the bathroom, and said, "We'll worry about that later. Let's take a look around the house, and kill anyone that doesn't belong here." We ended up in a bedroom we shared, and drilled a tiny hole in the wall. We placed a glass cup over the hole, and eavesdropped on Andrade, Pryce, and Ms. Brown.

We created a volume enhancing device, and successfully squeezed Andrade's voice through the hole in the wall. Ms. Brown reviewed Andrade's manuscript with a critical eye, and returned it to him. Andrade said, "So, what do you think?"

She smiled, and said, "Don't hesitate to use 12-syllable-English-words in your manuscript as long as you think your audience can ascertain the meaning through the context of your work."

Andrade said, "What you mean?"

She smirked, and said, "Antidisestablishmentarianism?"

Andrade said, "The 28 letter word is probably one of the longest words in the English language," and exhaled a thick cloud of marijuana smoke.

"You should market a screenplay to television producers, and the like."

Andrade said, "Breaking into Hollywood requires that I know someone who knows someone." He held a grenade in his hand with a ring around his finger. "First of all, the script needs to be purchased… producing a new series concept requires the talents of a casting director, cinematographer, location scout, sound mixer, and much more. In other words, the script has to be bankable."

"You can always target executive producers, and email them query letters."

Andrade shook his head in disagreement, and said, "Network executives, and executive producers receive countless query letters on a daily basis. There are over 8,500 professional screenwriters, and hundreds of aspiring screenwriters in America... a substantial underrepresented majority of unpublished authors submit their work to television producers with a signed release form, and commonly receive rejection slips in the mail."

"What's a release form?"

Andrade tilted his head, and said, "Mr. Pryce can answer that!"

Pryce exhaled cigarette smoke in the air, and said, "A release form makes clear to the television writer that his or her idea is nothing new to their studio executives, and an identical story-line may appear on television before his or her own eyes."

"Its termed simultaneous creation," Andrade stated. "We have all the right ingredients, and recipes to produce a publishable work of fiction. For example, characterization, narration, dialogue, and so forth. If, that makes sense."

"You should copyright it."

Pryce laughed, and said, "Copyright laws do not protect ideas. Neither, does the universal copyright convention in non-participating countries."

"Have you ever heard of a development deal?"

Andrade scratched his head, and said, "Absolutely! A studio purchases the licensing rights of a best-selling book, and employs a professional scriptwriter to expand the best-selling novel into a script. The scriptwriter is typically paid in the low millions, and works exclusively for the studio."

"A well-written query letter distributed to acquisition editors describing yourself, and the manuscript should yield positive results among trade publishers. Don't you think?"

Pryce said, "That all depends on who you talk to," and winked his eye. "A small publisher is more likely to deal with a first-time author than the larger New York houses would be. That's for sure!"

"What's a small publisher?"

Pryce said, "A publishing house with under $50 million in annual sales."

Ms. Brown said, "Wow! That's a lot of money." Andrade continued laughing, and she said, "What's so funny?"

Pryce said, "A medium-sized publishing house generates under a $100 million in annual revenue. A large-sized publishing house normally sites revenues of $50 million or greater per quarter, and published big-name authors with advances against future royalties."

Brown was amazed, and said, "Self-publishing is a prestigious pursuit, and would help you print, and bind your literary work. The world's brightest authors published their own material at one time or another, and left a footprint in the industry."

Andrade used an alcohol based hand sanitizer to limit the number of microbes on his hands. "Some folks are crazy enough to publish their own work under their own imprint, and pocket the proceeds themselves instead of accepting a royalty arrangement from a commercial publisher. It requires investment capital, entrepreneurial spirit, commitment, creativity, critical thinking skills, and a college degree."

Pryce remarked, "Well said."

"Thank you."

"Let's backtrack!" Pryce stated. "Editors normally ask their sales department to calculate sales orders for the proposed book, and the number of copies a major retailer would purchase around the globe. If, their sales department firmly believes the book is unmarketable, then the [expletive] book doesn't see the light of day. Andrade has been offered numerous boilerplate contracts, and has declined every single one with confidence."

She asked, "What's a boilerplate contract?"

Andrade leaned back in his chair. "Pryce can answer that!"

Pryce cleared his throat with an audible noise. "A publishing contract that's negotiable, and revised until both parties are happy. It gives the publishing house the right to publish, and distribute the literary work on agreed-upon soil. It spells out the author's obligations as well as the publishers, and sketches the monetary arrangements in esoteric words."

She stated, "Negotiating a publishing contract seems rather complicated, don't you think?"

Pryce used a toothpick to remove food detritus from his teeth, and said, "Maybe to a lawyer that doesn't specialize in publishing, but, there are significant elements that should not be overlooked, such as, international publication rights, subsidiary rights, foreign sales, option clauses, bankruptcy clauses, audit clauses, advances, and royalties. In a typical publishing agreement, the author basically grants the house the exclusive right to edit, print, publish, market, and license the rights to all formats of the final product in the English language throughout the universe."

She said, "Really?" With rising intonation.

Andrade exhaled marijuana smoke through his nostrils. "One thing an author should never do, and no matter how desperate he or she is to publish their work, is sell their book rights."

She asked, "What do you suggest?"

Andrade was putting pen to paper, and said, "Wait a minute," and continued writing his ideas between the lines. He finally closed the wirebound notebook, and said, "They should license the rights, so, he or she may continue to own it for the life of the copyright, which lasts 70 years after his or her death."

She said, "How do advances work?"

Pryce moved one hand to his chin, and began a chin-stroking gesture. "The author has to sign on the dotted line to receive the first payment, and submit the final manuscript to receive an additional payment. However, the publisher needs to verify that his or her work is publishable, and marketable before a check is printed out.

She asked, "Can the publisher terminate the contract?"

Pryce grinned. "Their contracts include language that enables their house to decline a manuscript as unpublishable, and force the author to repay them any sums advanced to him or her."

"So, they can pull the plug at any time?"

Pryce nodded his head. "Pretty much!"

"Can an author publish whatever he or she wants?"

Pryce said, "Not really."

"Why is that?"

Andrade said, "Some publishers carry libel insurance, but, libeling, slandering, and evading someone's privacy is a big mistake. If legal action emerges from the publication of a novel, and [expletive] hits the fan. Someone is going to be held accountable, and would need to hire a legal team that knows publishing law. It's that simple."

"You know what I would do If I were you?"

Andrade shook his head, and said, "No! What would you do?"

"Send multiple queries to reputable literary agents who sell books in your field, and attend every book convention around the world to promote your work."

Andrade massaged his forehead, and said, "Pryce what do you think?"

Pryce said, "Anticipate an agency clause in the agreement, and your checks to be mailed to the name of the agent printed in the publishing contract."

Andrade soaked a cigarette in phencyclidine, and said, "An intelligent agent would retain foreign rights on his client's behalf, and attempt to sell them to non-domestic publishers for a pretty penny, then divide the monies earned from the translation rights with the author."

Pryce started laughing, and Ms. Brown said, "What the [expletive] is so funny?"

Pryce said, "Some [expletive] contracts prohibit authors from signing a dissimilar contract with a competitor until his or her work is published."

"What's so funny about that?"

Andrade said, "Publication can be years after the manuscript is submitted to the publishing house."

"That's good to know. Especially, if someone is planning on working in the publishing sector as an author."

Pryce asked, "Do you want to know something else that's funny?"

"What?"

Pryce said, "A word count, and page count is specified in a publishing contract."

"That's interesting."

"So, is astrology," Andrade stated.

"What's that supposed to mean?"

Pryce said, "Never mind him."

"Is it true, a publisher has a contractual right to dictate the book's title, artwork, and the text on the back cover?"

Andrade said, "Pretty much…They are holding all the cards in the deck. The text on the back cover is a brief summary of the literary work, or is about the author."

Pryce said, "The house's acquisition editor normally reviews the final manuscript, and attaches his or her questions, comments, and proposed changes to an email that's sent to the author.

She said, "Wait a minute! What if the author dis-
agrees with the proposed changes, and is reluctant
to make the changes specified in the email?"

Andrade remained conscious with a staring
glaze. "The author is not going to get his or her
hands on a paycheck, and will probably be out of
a job in the unforeseeable future. A developmental
editor can make the changes as the acquisition editors sees fit, and reorganize the manuscript to meet
the house's expectations."

She remarked, "There's a lot more work involved in the production of a book than most people realize!"

Andrade said, "Its time consuming, but, worth
the effort, if, a sales representative has national accounts, and can convince national chains to purchase copies."

She said. "I can envision a sales rep handing over
sales sheets, and valuable information to national
chains on your behalf to persuade them to purchase

advance orders of your work."

Andrade said, "I'll take that as a compliment. Thank you."

Pryce said, "Stores order what they think they will sell in the first 13 days."

"Publishers can pay to have their author's work on counter displays, and endcaps to increase the chances of survival," Andrade said.

Pryce said, "We have a lot of work to do," and finished smoking his cigarette.

"You guys are a brilliant combination, and are going to make a ton of cash in the publishing industry. I will leave you two alone. I am going to look for Virula."

Andrade glanced at the pint-sized hole in the wall. "He's next door, and listening to everything we've discussed so far."

"How do you know?"

Andrade didn't answer her question, and Pryce said, "Don't forget to close the door on your way out. Thank you!"

CHAPTER 4

—◁◁◁◁◁⋯⋯▷▷▷▷▷—

I fixated on past mistakes, and ruminated over a failed relationship I experienced with Ms. Hanes. I read a letter I received from her at the county jail the day before I pleaded no contest to driving under the influence, and agreed to the criminal justice's diversion program on drug charges. I broke down, and cried. I was arrested after being pulled over for failing to stop at a stop sign, and refusing to take a breathalyzer test. The arresting officer drove me to a local hospital in handcuffs, and I unwillingly submitted to a blood alcohol test. I had a blood alcohol content of 0.16.

The arresting officer also found 1.1 grams of

cocaine in the glove compartment, and a firearm that had been reported stolen. My driver's license was suspended for 11 months, and I was ordered to complete 101 hours of community service. I was placed under probation supervision after serving a six month jail sentence, and received a wide range of unwanted rehabilitative services. For instance, mental health counseling, drug counseling, and educational programs tied to various court fees. I couldn't leave that state without the courts authorization, and refrained from the use, possession, and sale of crack cocaine.

Ms. Brown closed the door behind her, and said, "Virula!"

I set the four page letter on fire, and said, "What?"

She paused, and said, "I forgot what I was going to say." She unboxed the Ouija board on a levitated table, and said, "It takes two to tango."

A ghostly resident walked through a solid wall

adorned with demon-faced wallpaper, and said, "You got that right." A musical spirit pounded his finger tips on a see-through dust covered pipe-organ, and the ghost resident danced the waltz 2 feet off the hardwood floor. He said, "Get the 1-2-3 beat in your mind," as wispy specters flew out of 6,000 pipes with 5 manuals, 420 ranks, 310 registers, and 210 stops.

"Who is going to be the medium?"

She said, "I am," and positioned the planchette in the center of the Ouija board.

"Good, because I am having second thoughts about this [expletive]."

She said, "Place two fingers on the planchette."

I shrugged both shoulders, and said, "Alright, here goes nothing!"

"Now, concentrate." She asked a simple question that required a yes or no answer, and patiently waited for the spirit to response.

"This is silly."

"Give the spirit some time to respond," she said.

Nothing happened, so, she tried asking another question. We agreed to ask the spirit's name, and waited a minute for an answer to arrive. The planchette spelled R-I-C-H-A-R-D R-A-M-E-R-I-Z.

"Where were you born?"

The planchette spelled E-L P-A-S-O T-E-X-A-S.

"How old are you?"

The planchette spelled F-I-F-T-Y F-O-U-R.

"What year did you die?"

The planchette spelled T-W-O T-H-O-U-S-A-N-D T-H-I-R-T-E-E-N.

"How did you die?"

The planchette spelled B-C-E-L-L L-Y-M-P-H-O-M-A.

"Do you have a nickname?"

The planchette covered the three letter word 'YES' on the Ouija board.

"What is it?"

The planchette spelled T-H-E N-I-G-H-T S-T-A-L-K-E-R.

Ms. Brown was appalled, and said, "You are moving it!"

"No, you are moving it!"

"There is only one way to find out," and with an apprehensive smile, she said, "Who the [expletive] is in the other room?"

We withdrew our fingers from the device simultaneously, and the oracle spelled out T-W-O M-A-S-T-E-R-M-I-N-D-S. She thanked the spirit for being in attendance, and communicating with us through the board. A very raspy, wispy voice said, "Someone should write down the answers, because the letters spell out briskly, and it's difficult to keep track of what's being said."

A bisque porcelain doll sprinted across the room with a knife, and the planchette rested on the word 'GOODBYE.' The Ouija board caught on fire, and the bisque porcelain doll stabbed a large sized long tailed black haired rat to death. I said, "That was entertaining."

Espinoza bolted into the room with Fernandez in militaristic attire, and three-point slings attached to automatic weapons. He shouted, "We made it!"

"What the [expletive] is going on? What the [expletive] did you guys do?"

Espinoza was out of breath. Fernandez spoke up, "We robbed a financial institution, and got away with the money!"

"Have you lost your [expletive] mind?"

I utilized Fernandez's impetus, and carried him on his way to the ground. I said, "Run that by me again, I'm hard of hearing… what did you guys do, again?"

Fernandez said, "We robbed a bank."

I grinned, and said, "You guys robbed a bank?"

Espinoza looked like he had seen a ghost, and said, "It was Morales's idea!"

"Where [expletive] is he?"

Fernandez said, "He didn't make it!"

"What do you mean?"

Fernandez said, "Morales used a bank employee as a human shield, and opened fire on a squadron of officers in a minute-long gun battle."

"And?"

"And, he died," Fernandez said.

Espinoza said, "We led the authorities on a high-speed chase that lasted almost 21 minutes, and managed to shootout their Charles Goodyear tires. Fernandez shot at the police helicopter's fuel tank multiple times, and coerced the pilot to make an emergency landing at a local public airport."

"You got to be kidding me?" I acknowledged the rotor noise of a helicopter circling incessantly over-head, and said, "You're not kidding."

Authorities set up a perimeter, and a clean shaved field commander shouted, "Come out with your hands up," over the speaker. "I know you're in there! Come out with your hands up."

"There is a global positioning system device hidden in one of the packets of cash the teller handed you," I said.

Espinoza said, "How do you know?"

Fernandez smacked him upside the head, and said, "The cops are here fool!"

"Why did you rob a financial institution?"

Espinoza said, "That's where the money is!"

"Who the [expletive] do you think you are, Willie Sutton?"

Espinoza was clueless. "Who the [expletive] is that?"

"A legendary bank robber you idiot."

Fernandez asked, "So, what do we do? The incident commander is going to request the most elite tacticians of their department, and the designated law enforcement team is going to try to earn a commendation."

A 40mm liquid agent barricade projectile round flew through the window, and I said, "Looks like the special unit is already here."

Ms. Brown coughed uncontrollably, and said, "This is going to make the headlines!"

Espinoza shouted, "They are not taking me alive," and exited the room. He confronted the officers, and died on the driveway.

Fernandez's eyelids swelled up as lachrymator irritated his eyes, and created blinding tears. The liquid chemical agent behaved aerodynamically, and remained in the room for almost 30 seconds.

The clean shaven field commander shouted,

"This is the police department. Come out with your hands up! This is the last warning or the dogs will bite you," over the speaker.

I stepped up to the window, and yelled, "Who's going to hell with me?" I had a full magazine, and fired 11 shots out the window. I killed a canine, and left two officers in critical condition. Residents were forced to evacuate their homes, and gunshots rang out. The police closed a nearby intersection, and the air unit continued circling the neighborhood.

Snipers were positioned on adjacent roofs, and waiting for the right time to pull the trigger. Garcia, Lopez, and Marquez stormed in the room with military weapons, and exchanged gunfire with the police.

"Where did you guys come from?"

Garcia shouted, "We were down the street, and thought we should give you guys a hand."

"Boy, am I glad to see you!"

A ballistic armored tactical vehicle parked in front of the eight foot tall rusty old wrought iron dual driveway gate. "Looks like we got company."

I escorted Andrade, and Pryce to the subterranean passage snaking 1760 yards. "Follow him!" I shouted.

Ms. Brown said, "No! I want to be with you."

I didn't argue, and said, "Dammit! Follow me!"

De La Cruz met us in the hallway, and followed us to the room. "Have you ever heard of adverse possession?"

Bullets were flying in every direction, and made the wall behind us look worse than the El Badi Palace in Marrakech. I ducked down, and said, "Nope."

De La Cruz ducked his head, and said, "Well, I brought a lawsuit to a quiet title, and the court settled who owns the estate."

Gun shots rang out, and I said, "Can we talk

about this some other time?"

De La Cruz said, "I just wanted to tell you that we have to pay property taxes," and he died from gun inflicted wounds.

I heard patrol units whizzing down the street, and the clean shaven field commander shout, "Come out with your hands up. This is the police department. This is the last warning. Come out with your hands up."

I poked my head out the window, and yelled, "Not a chance! I'm leaving in a body bag! So, what are you waiting for? Come in!"

Lopez said, "They are probably waiting for a search warrant to enter the house."

"That's… highly unlikely."

"What do you think there doing?" asked Garcia.

Marquez scratched his head. "Ask, Virula. He's the smartest one in the room."

"Do me a favor," I asked.

Garcia said, "What?"

"Pick up the phone, and tell me what you hear."

"That's funny... I don't hear a dial tone," Garcia said.

"Wait!"

"Wait, for what?"

"For someone to answer the other line."

A voice responded. "This is commander Seagal of the Los Angeles County sheriff's office."

Garcia said, "Hold on! I have someone here that would like to speak with you."

"Put'em on the line," the commander responded.

Garcia placed the phone at the end of his alimentary canal, and farted.

Marquez was startled. "How did you know that was going to happen?"

"I didn't! It was an educated guess. At this point, the law enforcement agency has already contacted the telecommunications company, and asked the company to prohibit outgoing calls from our location."

Lopez said, "They can do that?"

"Sure they can! The only thing a law enforcement agent needs to do is contact the telephone company, and provide our address. That's how they did it. If, you pick up the phone again, it is going to automatically ring the number to commander Seagal."

Marquez said, "Can the commander contact us?"

"I'm sure he can."

The phone rang, and Marquez answered, "Hello." He lowered the phone, and said, "It's the commander. What do we do?"

Lopez stood at the window, and yelled, "I'll tell you what we need to do," and struck several officers with gunfire. He stumbled backwards a few steps, and dropped dead from gun inflicted wounds.

Garcia shouted, "We're out numbered. We need to get the [expletive] out of here."

Ms. Brown stood up, and was struck by a burst of semi-automatic gunfire. I held her in my arms, and said, "I'm sorry!"

Spitting up blood, she said, "I love you."

"I love you too," and she died. I looked at Fernando, "This is all your [expletive] fault," and shot him twice in the chest.

Marquez shouted, "I'm getting the [expletive] out of here," and exited the room with Garcia. Law enforcement agents forced entry into the house, and found me talking to Ms. Brown in my arms. I was taken for a mental health evaluation, and in police custody soon after. I was under the influence of hallucinogens the whole time.

'Now, I am spending the rest of my life in prison,

talking endlessly about my past.... to cellmates that share their life stories with me. Some stories are insipid, and some are worth writing down, like this one.'

My cellmate serving 30 years for bank robbery dangles his feet off the steel bunk bed, and says, "Man! That was one hell of a story. Tell it again."